# Justice Marshall

## Fighter for Equality

**Jeri Cipriano**

PEARSON

Boston, Massachusetts
Chandler, Arizona
Glenview, Illinois
Upper Saddle River, New Jersey

**Illustrations**
6, 8, 9, 12 L. R. Galante.

**Photographs**
Every effort has been made to secure permission and provide appropriate credit for photographic material. The publisher deeply regrets any omission and pledges to correct errors called to its attention in subsequent editions.

Unless otherwise acknowledged, all photographs are the property of Pearson Education, Inc.

Photo locators denoted as follows: Top (T), Center (C), Bottom (B), Left (L), Right (R), Background (Bkgd)

Opener: *U.S. News & World Report Magazine* Collection/Library of Congress; 1 (T) *U.S. News & World Report Magazine* Collection/Library of Congress; 2 (B) *U.S. News & World Report Magazine* Collection/Library of Congress; 3 (T) U.S. Farm Security Administration/Office of War Information Black & White Photographs/Library of Congress; 4 (B) Prints & Photographs Division, Smith, William Morris, Selected Civil War photographs, 1861-1865 /Library of Congress; 5 (T) Comstock/Thinkstock; 7 (B) Library of Congress; 10 (T) Image courtesy of the South Carolina Department of Archives and History; 11 (B) Image courtesy of the South Carolina Department of Archives and History; 13 (B) *U.S. News & World Report Magazine* Photograph Collection, Bledsoe, John T./Library of Congress; 14 (T) LBJ Library photo by Frank Wolfe /Lyndon Baines Johnson Library; 15 (R) ©Ellen Isaacs/Alamy.



ISBN-13: 978-0-328-67609-5
ISBN-10: 0-328-67609-8

2 3 4 5 6 V0FL 16 15 14 13 12

# Doing Good for Others

Do you think one person can change the lives of many people for the better? Thurgood Marshall did. Marshall worked as a lawyer and then as a judge. He took part in many important court cases. He helped make sure all Americans had equal rights.

During segregation, many places had separate drinking fountains for African Americans and for white Americans.

Marshall grew up in the early 1900s. Things were very different then. In some parts of the country, especially the South, **segregation** laws kept black and white people apart. African Americans could not go to the same schools as whites. They had separate stores and restaurants, too. These laws were based on beliefs some people had that whites were better than blacks.

Marshall knew these laws went against the United States **Constitution**. The Constitution says everyone should have equal protection under the law. As an adult, he worked to make sure the Constitution was for everyone.

# Marshall's Family

Marshall was born on July 2, 1908, in Baltimore, Maryland. He was the grandson of a man named Thoroughgood Marshall who had been enslaved. His grandfather had fought in the **Civil War**. Marshall was named after him. But the name was too long. He shortened it to Thurgood when he was just six years old.

Marshall's mother was a teacher. His father worked as an assistant at an all-white men's club. His father taught him many things that helped him when he became a lawyer.

Many African American men fought for the North during the Civil War in the 1860s.

Marshall and his father often talked about things that were going on in the world. They didn't always agree. Marshall's father taught him how to win arguments by using solid facts, not opinions. His father also took him to courtrooms to see trials. Marshall saw firsthand how lawyers worked.

In school, Marshall sometimes got in trouble. His teachers punished him. They made him copy parts of the Constitution. Soon Marshall had it memorized.

# Hard Lessons

The Constitution says all Americans should be treated equally under the law. But Marshall saw that blacks were often treated unfairly. One time when he was a teenager, Marshall got on a trolley car. Trolley cars moved people around cities like buses or trains do today. A white man on the trolley lied and started a fight. He claimed that Marshall had stepped ahead of a white woman.

No one would take Marshall's side. The police came and took him away. Marshall was lucky. His boss, a white man, found him. His boss told the police to let Marshall go.

After high school, Marshall went to Lincoln University. This was an all-black college in Pennsylvania. One day he and some other students went to a movie theater. They were told to sit in the balcony. That was the section for black people.

Marshall and his friends refused to sit in the black section. Standing up for their rights was dangerous. The students could have been jailed or beaten. But there was only one police officer in town. The jail was too small to hold all the students. But this experience convinced Marshall he needed to do something to change the laws and help African Americans.

Howard University

# Becoming a Lawyer

After graduating college, Marshall wanted to go to law school. He liked the University of Maryland. It was near his home. However, the school would not accept him because he was black. Instead, he went to Howard University in Washington, D.C.

Marshall could not afford to live in Washington. Every day he took a train at 5 A.M. from Baltimore to Washington. He would get home close to midnight. In 1933 he graduated first in his class.

One of Marshall's first big cases as a lawyer involved a man named Donald Murray. The University of Maryland would not let Murray attend classes because he was black. This was the same college that did not allow Marshall in. Murray and Marshall took the university to court. Marshall won the case. By law, the school had to let Murray attend.

During the 1940s and 1950s, Marshall became one of the country's best lawyers. He worked throughout the South fighting for the rights of African Americans.

Donald Murray (left) and Thurgood Marshall (right)

A white school in Paxville, South Carolina

## The Biggest Case

Marshall's most important case was about segregated public schools. Courts allowed separate schools for black and white children as long as they were equal. Marshall had to prove that separate schools were never equal. He needed to show that the education received by African American children was not as good because of segregation.

Marshall's case went all the way to the **Supreme Court**. He invited **experts** to present the facts about segregated schools. The experts said that local governments gave more money to white schools. Black schools were often run-down. They were overcrowded and had fewer supplies. Studies showed that a poor education made African American children feel less important than whites.

A black school in the same town

Marshall celebrated after winning the Supreme Court case.

# No More Segregation

May 17, 1954, was the day the Supreme Court gave its ruling. Separate schools were not equal. Marshall had won!

The Supreme Court said that blacks were not treated the same as whites. Segregation in public schools was declared illegal. The ruling would one day lead to the end of segregation in shops, restaurants, and other places.

Over the next few years, African American students began going to white schools. But many white people did not like this. They fought the changes.

In 1960, Ruby Bridges became the first African American to go to a white elementary school in New Orleans, Louisiana. Every day, she had to walk past angry, yelling crowds at the school. Officers were sent to protect her. Over time, things got better. Segregation ended in most public schools.

Some white people protested the end of school segregation.

President Johnson (right) with Marshall in 1967

# To the Supreme Court

As a lawyer, Marshall continued to fight for equal rights. Many more of his cases went to the Supreme Court. He won 29 of the 32 cases he brought before the Court. This record has never been broken.

In 1967, President Lyndon Johnson named Marshall to the Supreme Court. He became the first African American to become a **justice** on the Court. He served with eight other justices.

Marshall served on the Supreme Court for 24 years. He left the Court in 1991 because of poor health. He died in 1993 at the age of 84. Many people remember Thurgood Marshall as someone who helped make the world a better place. He fought for equal rights for all Americans.

# Glossary

**Civil War** the war fought from 1861 to 1865 between the northern and southern states of the United States

**Constitution** the document that is the plan for the United States government, and the highest law in the country

**expert** a person with special skills or knowledge in a subject

**justice** a judge

**segregation** the separation of people of different races

**Supreme Court** the highest court in the United States